GOOD
BYE
WOLF

the operating system digital//document

Goodbye Wolf

ISBN # 978-1-946031-71-6
Library of Congress Cataloguing-in-Publication # 9781946031716
copyright © 2020 by Nik De Dominic
edited & designed by Andrew Wessels & ELÆ [Lynne DeSilva-Johnson]

is released under a Creative Commons CC-BY-NC-ND (Attribution, Non Commercial, No Derivatives) License: its reproduction is encouraged for those who otherwise could not afford its purchase in the case of academic, personal, and other creative usage from which no profit will accrue.

Complete rules and restrictions are available at:
http://creativecommons.org/licenses/by-nc-nd/3.0/

For additional questions regarding reproduction, quotation, or to request a pdf for review contact operator@theoperatingsystem.org

This text was set in Brandon Grotesque, Minion Pro, Arnhem, Franchise, and OCR-A Standard.

Your donation makes our publications, platform and programs possible!
We <3 You.

bit.ly/growtheoperatingsystem

the operating system
www.theoperatingsystem.org
operator@theoperatingsystem.org

GOOD BYE WOLF

nik de dominic

GOOD BYE WOLF

Your Daily Horoscope

The Mayans called.
They want their calendar back.

Some say the stars
are a scam. That I sell snake oil

and lullabies. I say we believe
whatever we want to believe.

A man will email,
it may be me, saying

he's of a distant relation,
that if you give him a dollar

he will return it tenfold.
Do it this time just to see

what happens. I have faith
in our spectacular possibility.

Dear Wolf:

Janna says *Los Angeles* like Judy Garland or someone flying in with a couple of keys, two Es to a Z. I'm not sure where she picked it up. Neither of us despite living in New Orleans for ten years knows how to say New Orleans. In New Orleans, people never turn an age. They make that age. How old you make? I made 21. Life not passive, a birthday an achievement. Maybe something about the French verb *faire* and the same way people *make groceries*. But the French is 'to have.' *I have 21 years*. Here I mention something about disease. The doctor says it sounds a lot scarier than it is: lung disease. Here I think about breath. To breathe. Again. And how. A meditation tape tells me to focus on the breath, its irregularity, boy howdy. I wonder if how we say a place changes the place. I wonder if how we say a place changes a place. Change this place.

Your Daily Horoscope

On the Chinatown bus, a woman will witness you.
I prayed to Jesus for girls, and they kept coming:
Tony and Dennis and Tyler and Troy and Reggie.

You won't question this. A man next to you will study
a manila folder full of xeroxes of handwritten notes.
Childlike scrawl, every letter drawn over and over itself

so that Ys look like trees stricken by cat's claw
and wisteria reminding you of the south you left. There is
a crude circle cut in triangles, each an astrological sign:

the sign under which Christ was born and Abraham too.
Simple reckoning in the marginalia, the constant
mention of the Mayans, their calendar.

A note: my heart is broken in 3 halves.
When films were made and under which moon,
The Wizard of Oz (1939).

You would ask questions if you this weren't a stranger,
you not on the bus reading
over his shoulder. A child will fall into your lap

at an abrupt stop. Your stop.
At the corner, Jehovah's Witnesses will hand out pamphlets—
Is Satan Real?

A kid with a diamond tipped scribe will etch his name
in the storefront glass of the mostly costume jewelry shop
until the owner bangs on the window.

Make your way to work,
say hello to Sabrina,
Google the Scarecrow, him torn apart.

Dear Wolf:

Early mapmakers thought the world equitable
for every animal on land its counterpart at sea

sea horse, sea bear, sea pig
their world known only by lore and tale

in every uncharted expanse
exist monsters

a horse with the tail of a serpent
mermaids and men

a spinney whale of two spouts
while Poseidon plays his lute

gods wrestle each other
what is unknown is threat

tales to tell of tails
cavities come from tooth worms

your happiness promoted by spleen and humors
lay back and let us leech

sickness by bloodlet
how different this then

from yours Dear Wolf?
To test for magic and spell

what is unknown is monster.

Your Daily Horoscope

The stars and planets will not affect
your life in any way. It's true.

The Voice is on at 7 and I'm eating nachos.
We have a trainer for our dog

because it's "leash aggressive."
This is not entirely true:

it's just fucking aggressive.
A Katrina dog, street puppy.

Today on the internet someone shares:
Tinder for dogs. It's like real life but better.

Single white corgi mix seeks same for
no strings attached fun (must be fixed).

Long, silent stares across blocks, sleeping
on dirty laundry. Some intimacy issues.

Someone shares one of the guys from *Car Talk* died today
and a young girl with terminal cancer killed herself.

The Brazilian student-teacher sex-tape is a hoax,
not a student and not a teacher. An attractive man

in Santa Cruz beat a man with an umbrella
for wearing a Fox News costume on Halloween

and the internet has a new sexiest mug-shot contender,
soon his face shopped into Givenchy ads.

The stars and planets will not affect
your life in anyway. None of this will.

Dear Wolf:

I buy donuts after procedures from the fancy donut place, my special treat. The donuts are four bucks a pop, vegan, and named puns of rock bands—that's how fancy it is—like the yo la mango (yo la tengo) or banana kill (bikini kill) or gg almond... Everyone in the waiting room of the imaging lab is old and dying and I wonder why they're trying so hard. Everyone is on their cell phones, talking to kids and loved ones: *We're in LA for Dad's procedure*, dad's wife says. A couple minutes later, Dad and I are scheduled in rooms next to each other and he's naked under gown bumbling around the radiology control panel, pissing off the tech, looking for a pen for god knows what. Dad looks like he was old when Kennedy was in office and couldn't find his bellybutton if you asked him to. What will his MRI find, that he's dying? Dad knows that. Today I'm here for a CT scan where they will fill me with iodine and warm my body from the inside like a strange brandy drunk: first my brain, then my groin and belly, and finally appendages, as the axial x-ray spins around me like a giant rotisserie. I chant in sync with the rhythm of the machine's hum and its instructions to breathe, I am a jelly donut.

Your Daily Horoscope

Someone will send you a .gif
of a clown tying a noose
around his neck to a sapling.
He will then water the sapling.
Everywhere a .gif a gift.

Dear Wolf:

The river is swollen
and laps the banks.
The boat is wet.
I hate this damn boat.

The river is a snake
and laps the banks.
The boat is wet.
I hate this damn boat.

The river is a swollen snake
and laps the banks & writhes.
The river a swollen pregnant snake.
A storm coming.

The sea infinite
its heaving
rainfull & kisses
the snake's hatchlings.

They are covered in wet black.
Too young they don't know
how to feed:
mice living,

the babies play.

Your Daily Horoscope

Someone will share an article
about a dog's gaze, why we bond
with it like a child. Rover's look
releases oxytocin. The cuddle chemical
encourages bonding between
mothers and offspring
and also responsible for coupling.
Someone else will ask
what happens if the dog's blind.
People are dicks.

Dear Wolf:

Sickness makes us children.
We wait. Always waiting.
Boredom again the defining characteristic
of our lives. An old couple bickers –
explains things to each other they mostly know.
Sometimes people talk to remove weight.
We echo. I ask Janna what she thinks
of the 13 year old Louisiana soul singer on *The Voice*.
I like her, she says.
Me too. Intake asks me up
and I want to tell him I've always
thought Adam Levine was a sleaze
or that the iron in my blood is just dead
stars or I will miss him when I'm gone
like some sad pop song
but here we're reduced to birthdates
so I answer, One-oneone-eightyone.
Like a chorus, One-oneone-eightyone.
One-oneone-eightyone, I sing myself.

Your Daily Horoscope

Fall is finally here. Leaves
leafing and everywhere a'pumpkin
spice. Did you know there's no pumpkin
in pumpkin spice? I want you to think
about that today, Stargazer. And imagine
the latte. You are the latte. No, not foamy
and overpriced. But deceptive in your flavoring.
You may taste like one thing but you are
entirely a different thing. In this case, high-fructose
corn syrup. But that's neither here nor there.
Also, this – the latte exists in concentrate.
There is very little liquid milk there
before it's foamed and takes its shape.
There's something there, a science lesson,
for you: something about volume
and density and space. I'd tell you more
but that's for you to decipher this day
and I went to horoscope school.

Dear Wolf:

Imagine
you are
a retired geek:

Say bird
I miss
you

your head quivering
in my mouth
its tiny beak

little
convulsions before
and after

the way a crowd
gathers
and tenses

releases before
I spit
you a body limp

that love
can be so whole
fingers

wrapped
around a body
all body whole

body dear snake
your tongue
in mine

teeth teething
a tether
a snake

eating
a snake
so many

bodies
headless
littering and

without shape
a stage full of bones
so hollow and

full of applause.

Your Daily Horoscope

The Chinatown bus today
is unusually crowded.
The morning is a gun
metal gray and if you
look hard enough you
can see the circular striations
of where the hills were machined.
Everyone is on their cellphones
playing Farmville and Bejeweled,
and no one's volume muted.
The bus is a carnival ride
of self-interest. One guy
literally navel gazes.
You jockey for position
on the upper rail, find
a good spot and open
Facebook. None of the "People
You May Know" do you know,
but rather it's tiny pictures
of all the other bus passengers.
When everyone starts singing,
surprised, you know all the words.

Dear Wolf:

I remember when I was a kid
every other week some kid fell into a well.

My childhood's greatest threat was an earthen maw
with stone teeth yawning to darkness

where at the bottom a pit gut hungry for children
lived boys and girls that looked just like me.

They would lower food to us, radios, and tiny mirrors
 to flash back up so we could communicate by light.

I grew up in Los Angeles and had never even seen a well.
I have no idea why wells love children or

why so much has vanished.

Your Daily Horoscope

Well, Stargazer, today is your day.
Kind of. Imagine you just moved to a new region
and for the last six months you'd been applying
for jobs. Today every resume you sent
will be returned. All 8,000 of them.
When one call is done, the phone rings.
You pick it up, call waiting interrupts.
You get a notification on Facebook, then another.
Your Instagram photograph of a dog in tie has a 1,000 new likes.
Cute picture, one writes. Want to come work for us?
Your email pings. And then again. And again.
They begin to sense your fraying
and like teenage lovers become incensed:
What, you don't want to work for us? Fine.
No, that's not what I mean, hold on, one second,
you say. The comments become angry.
Soon they are all at your front door,
pitchforks, torches, gnawing at each other,
throwing out offers, benefits, matching 401ks.
Before the riot, you shutter the windows,
put your phone into airplane mode and go
back to bed. The covers are cool to the touch,
and you dream of riding an endless escalator endlessly.

Dear Wolf:

You're the body it awakes
this violent body awoke
the animal stretch and lungyawn of morning
already the morning how troubling my body has become
the splintered skin an emptied vessel
the joint inflamed here the coupled yoke
a connection a place of convergence and touch
how skin covers muscle covered bone
and every organ is suspect ready willing stretched
to turn a devil inside here a field an opening
you're the body it takes imagining the body
a machine tilling soil turning itself on itself over itself
oxen plow field dawned a child's prayer rolled over
and over on the tongue in the mouth vowelfat
as words until they become meaningless like this body
and are only lightly associated to something like touch
just out of reach - the word a light touch uncoupled
no vehicle no tenor now I lay me down to sleep.

Your Daily Horoscope

Today, Stargazer, unfortunately, everything will break. Horoscope, from the Latin, literally, time observer. You are the watcher. Today, Stargazer, time will break. So will teeth and bone and nail. Infrastructures will crumble. Blood in the streets. The dog will yowl. First, meteors, then fire, then as they say, all hell will break loose.

This is all ok, Stargazer.

Reading your charts, I can say this would be a good time to take personal inventory and decide what it is most important to you so that you may stockpile it in your survivalist uncle's bunker in the desert off i90.

Bring those peanut butter cookies I like.
The ones from Trader Joe's.

Dear Wolf:

Here is where the rubber meets
the pavement or the tires
meet the road or my hands

meet gravel or whatever the expression.
There is only gravel and glass
in your scalp, under our fingernails.

Maybe. I have shown you
this wound, the hand
where the skin was taken

left here to her where something
not quite what was has grown
over it and when I rub my finger

over the wound the palm I know
something is missing. What is here
is what was left but not what was.

I can never describe an accident
because it was an accident.

Your Daily Horoscope

Dr. John sang, *Your steak ain't no hipper than my pork chop,*
your Cadillac no hipper than my bus stop, your champagne no hipper

than my soda pop. I don't know if I agree with him
unless he cooks a really good pork chop, sure,

but really, champagne and soda isn't a useful comparison.
They are totally different things – one's got booze in it –

and Dr. John is ugly as fuck.
What I do want you to take from this, Stargazer, is I was born

in the #12 St. Louis cemetery at midnight in New Orleans birthed
by 12 midwifes to 12 fathers in a litter of 12.

No one cried, no one celebrated. The moon and 12 stars pricked
my eyes open early, all the other kittens staying dumb and blind

another 12 weeks. My kin were all picked off by a 12 pack
of opossum and I was the first to catch a sparrow

in my mouth to leave 12 feathers on your pillow
and I won't stop until another 12 I get.

Dear Wolf:

Entering light is reflected
at ninety degrees to passing
motorists. Reflectors mounted

at headlight height face across
the highway from each other
never directly across

from each other but offset.
Additional reflectors are required
where roadsides slope downward.

You mention parallax stars
how we can only see by looking away
how traffic slows when no one does.

Your Daily Horoscope

You have a moon in your second house,
Stargazer, and he's a terrible tenant.
Slovenly he doesn't work, watches
Ellen all day, slightly shimmying when she dances,
sits on the porch in the afternoon and leers
at the neighborhood kids on their Huffies in a way
that makes no one comfortable. Cocaine-fueled parties
every night, broken porcelain toilets and tubs.
The moon was moving through some financial problems
when he signed the lease so out of the kindness
of your heart you forewent deposit.
You don't even have that recourse.
You've called the county but eviction
in Star City is a slow moving process.

Dear Wolf:

We touch back like spark:
current cam current coil current.
Ask if I remember running suicides
in gym and tell me how horses
make their own steam.

Your Daily Horoscope

You will wake up today with a fifteen-year-old song in your head. When you shower, you will ceaselessly hum, your mouth full of toothbrush and pop notes, you will froth toothpaste all over your pubic hair. Walking the dog, on the bus, in the office, you won't shake it. You will doodle lyric on a company pad while making telemarketing calls to people you imagine in ren-faire biz casual – billowy skirts, riding boots, and transition lenses that no longer transition, stuck somewhere between baseball game and bedtime – so that they can renew their database subscriptions. After a particularly bad interaction with a CEO's gatekeeper, you will say: *I'm sorry, Miss Jackson, but I am for real. Thank you for your time, goodbye.* Later in the bathroom, while urinating, you will look at your genitals and apologize a million more times.

Dear Wolf:

Several years ago
on the highway between
Alabama and Louisiana

somewhere in Mississippi
I became unable to distinguish
dream from memory from reality

from place from place
from roadside fires and Waffle Houses
from the man-sized pines that litter

the highways of the southeast.
Places I'd never been I'd been before.
Fantastic things happened the night before:

you set fire to the cattle.
The whole field orange in the dark
the headlights of a passing truck.

I sleep too much
if I let myself
most the day away.

Disease makes us
the strangest
strangers.

A West Texas jackrabbit
pinned to the tank
of your Honda 250,

road kill found
and skinned lovingly
in Terlingua, the ghost town, unmarked

on the map and built around
the cinnabar mines.
Dragon's blood. Wounded monster.

The foot a good luck charm
to ward off bad spirits
and keep traffic moving,

the wind behind you.
A light rain brings the oil up
to the surface

the road grows slick.
Like the mercurialism
of a miner's death

the bike goes into shakes,
loses its memory, can't find its place
in the world and you

have to lay her down.
Problem with rabbits' feet
they aren't very lucky for rabbits.

Your Daily Horoscope

In the sawdust the children dance.
The children dance in the sawdust.

In red hood holding your sleeve,
you walk towards a man, your shadow.

Your feet kick up this dust. This earth
in shade clouds around.

In this field we will find each other.
We will find each other in this field.

Dear Wolf:

When you arrived we knew
you were unlike the others:
sickly and underweight, fur
a strange matte, full of burs.

I took you to my breast,
with the others, let you play rough
with the others but intervened
when too rough.

How you came naked and still,
abandoned, your smell sweet.
You had no taste for the blood
of fish, huckleberry, ants and wasps.

You are not growing, skin
loose. Naked but still clothed.
Small toothed and ugly, sex unsure.
I will weep for you as my own.

Your Daily Horoscope

You will get a note
that someone
important
died.
You will not
be able to place
the name
or relationship.
You will wake
up in a dream
where all your friends
are grieving.
They will all talk
in fake southern accents
and wear
phony black moustaches.
Even the women
like vaudevillian villains
and they will pretend
not to know you.
And you will say,
but it's me, it's me.
They will plan
a train robbery.
And tie you to the tracks.

Dear Wolf:

In the green and in the reed grass we tell secrets.
A light finger pressed to bowed mouth.

We say hush before a stone's skipped across
the fountain's surface.

Here, a wish. Here, a tree. Here, a statue:
a child saddling a tortoise.

I know your mouth, the stone says to water.
I know your limbs, the cat's claw says to tree.

Its trumpet our funeral creeper.
The Spanish moss lies about me, says tree, and tells the others

I say it's all going to be ok, that everyone will bring tulips
and leave them at the foot of our beds in the cement shade.

Says the child says that the marble's not so cold.
How could something so green suffocate.

This place always so full, always breathing.

Your Daily Horoscope

There is a beach. A party. A beach party. You come across this beach party and everyone is in formal wear. Everyone knows your name but you're unable to place theirs. Each face is a soft memory: the inside of a jacket, the backseat of a car, a meal in New Jersey waiting for a train, a shared key bump in a bathroom when you were 19, a class in grad school on Sir Gawain and the Green Knight, a street vendor hawking hot tamales in a neighborhood you left years ago. Maybe. You think. But they all know your name. They have read books on making friends and influencing people and they use your name like punctuation, like breathing, like metronome. Someone suggests lighting a fire but there is no wood, no kindling. You feel immense guilt for not remembering anyone's name and they all knowing yours, and since your clothes are not as a fine, up you offer them. They say thank you and strip you naked. Your underwear, jeans, and shirt lit in a small pile in the sand. They go up quickly in flames and reduce themselves to soft ash in a blue chemical burn. They look to you hungry when there is nothing left, so you give them your skin and fat. It drips, pops and sizzles into the sand, turning to tiny black dots like fossilized sea creatures in the grit. And your fat and skin are enough to cook off and keep them warm as the sun drops below the blanket of sea. Your memories of those attending the party become clearer and you are almost able to place one of them when your bones are tossed into the flame. They say, thank you, father. Do you remember me? They say, thank you, son. Do you remember me? You burn until there is nothing left. Sand, sea, and stars.

Dear Wolf:

The children on public broadcasting are defining
matter. They work through definitions, the familiar
stuff of daily life: it takes up space, has weight.
A man shows a kid a flash card—a tree.

You can pick up a tree, the kid says. It's matter.
Glass? Yes, matter. The next flash card—echo?
No. I cannot touch an echo. Air, the card says.
Air is the problem. The kid waffles. It is around us,

he says, space. He lifts his hands in front of his chest.
I can pick it up, he says. Maybe.
The kid takes a bicycle pump and fills a plastic bottle full.
He's asked by the scientist if it is matter. It is. I can feel it

expand. They weigh the bottle and the invisible alters.
A woman now teaches him the moon, matter—that that
out there just through the glass, beyond the tree, past
our laughter's echo, hung in air, all of this, matter.

Your Daily Horoscope

Things to be read: coffee grounds & tea-leaves & how you peel an orange & test results. If the rind rolls and curls as one or into many parts. Handwriting samples: the curve of an L, how far the J drops below, stains on the loose leaf of a love note. Overpopulation killed the Mayans. A carnival barker guesses your height and weight for 2 bucks. Stands you in front of a six-foot pole, asks you to pull your hair back, what your favorite coat looks like and which side of the bed you sleep. Misdirection. What you had for breakfast, lunch, if you've had rhubarb pie, if you know what rhubarb looks like. Things to be read: your handedness tells me your personality, the crook of your finger, the way you hold a pen. Where you place a stamp and write a return address, the stamp square or not, address in upper right or the back of an envelope. The earth's rotation is fastest at the equator. How many rings before you pick up the phone. Ask the gods where the water is, when it will come, how much rain we will see. How we need it. Roll the dice to see where we land, what we'll do, if happiness is hard-fought but still coming. What good fortune yields. What that means. The world is mostly flat — at least here in the valley. A tarot card reader's sign promises good fortune for all who enter with a twenty-dollar bill and a genial disposition. Specializes in some telepathy, mostly clairvoyance. Lightning keeps striking the same tree, split then split again to split again. Things to read: buoyancy in the bath, whether your hair sinks or floats around your skull, if you close your eyes when you lean back, how much you can see underwater. Imagine a penny dropped from the tallest building, how it drives itself fathoms deep into the surface of the earth.

Dear Wolf:

We must travel in this direction
away to go toward our destination.

You tell me your father believed
air travel was the greatest hoax

he knew man had perfected
teleportation and the tube we enter

the scenery ran by the windows
all keystone and pantomime.

I tell you flight reminds me
our bodies are containers.

It is the only time I know there are things
inside the skin and bone contained,

their gravity different than our own.

Your Daily Horoscope

The men will take you in the forest they come upon your tents in the night and take you sleeping from slumber in your sleep the men take you in the forest they come through the woods leaves under toes crushing and they take you sleeping from your slumber while you sleep the men take you trampling the ground with their feet they put their hands to your necks and take you from your sleeping forest in your tents the men take you they are covered in mud smeared on their faces across your faces the men take you in the forest when you sleep in your slumber and you keep close and tight in the night your back to another's as you sleep one of you always watchful with an eye toward the horizon you see the men coming to take you in the forest and there is not a damn thing anyone can do as the sun sets and someone nods off and the guard is lost to the night the men take you in the forest when they come upon your tents in the night putting their hands to your mouths the mud on the breath the glint of their knives in their eyes to your necks the men take you in the forest while you sleep in your slumber peacefully waiting always waiting for the men.

Dear Wolf:

The boy knows how many fingers you're holding behind your back.

The boy knows a number between one and thirty-six you hold in your mind's eye.

The boy knows the taste of mercury.

The boy knows how many toothpicks are in the jar—3,403.

The boy knows how many months before the lilac blooms.

The boy knows the pattern of the hawk moth's wings before it hatches.

The boy rolls its cocoon in his mouth to discern under his tongue.

The boy is careful not to chew.

The boy draws its outline in pencil on the wall.

The boy rubs the lead.

The boy knows how many studs in the wall.

The boy knows Arabic, French, English, Spanish and so on.

The boy knows your name but not his own.

Your Daily Horoscope

You build
to build
to build
a door
to a door
stairway to
stairway
how do
you enter
a place
with no
beginning
and con-
structed
without end
a closet opens
to a closet
inside a
small box
full of boxes:
a feather
a tooth
a shotgun shell
a fingernail.

Dear Wolf:

I write all my poems
on the back of photographs

of car accidents
place not important

but the surprise of entering
a familiar corner

at unfamiliar speed
the back wheels loosed.

Can you tell me again
how that forest caught fire

and that above its thick trees
to the east a column of black smoke smoked.

Everywhere a threat thread through.
Animals fled. Birds a murmuration and a black fox

paused on its paws picking a burr from its fur
with its muzzle. I am thinking of a word

between a thief and a lover
and nothing comes to mind

but you. I heard on the radio
that the wolf is no longer endangered

but before we celebrate
a pack of 7 in Siskiyou County

has disappeared. Your disease the same.
No news is good news, you keep saying, lover.

Thief at the door of your den
a request for my identity

my answer my passcode
zeroone oneone eightyone.

You are an imposter.
A mask different for each carnival.

Here, feathers at your face.
Here, a new tail.

Mask from witch,
specter thrown, say cast.

Today you are the crow, adorn
our nest with totem all I've grown

to know—glass jar of q-tips
a biohazard bin, cotton balls &

alcohol wipes, paper gowns,
sensicare powder free nitrile exam gloves,

super sani-cloth, & a WelchAllyn blood pressure
and temperature machine, the loving embrace

of its cuff, its release,
each bite a butterfly.

Your Daily Horoscope

Twenty years ago
Dizzy had some racket
with Impalas
and could have keys cut
to VIN numbers.
A perfumed icon
hanging from the rear view
as we drove around
doing crimes.
Now I ride the 794
to work and I think
Dizzy is dead.
Everyone on this line
infirmed somehow,
walkers and wheelchairs,
boils and bald,
reeks of salad dressing,
and I am trying to figure out
what my problem is.
Big and beautiful
blonde boys
bring their bibles
on the bus, sit closely
together in starched white
short shirt sleeves,
murmur to each other

the secrets of the after this.
Is it a bible, the thing Mormons
morm from? The strip-mall church
off San Fernando,
Pentecostal something or other,
is giving away food
and there is a line out the door,
up both sides of the block.
A little girl with black bangs hangs
in her parents' hands over a pack of pigeons,
brethren grieving
over a fallen and headless brother,
and she spits at them to scatter.
When I get home
still afternoon
we lie in bed and let the house go
from day to blue.
I tell you I read today
that you are everyone
in your dreams.
No shit, you say,
who else would you be.

Goodbye Wolf:

My mother sends me pictures
of herself. At first, I thought
this odd. I know what she
looks like. My father says
people do this when they think
they are dying, send things out
knick knacks from the attic,
baby pictures, ephemera.
My father says most people
think they are dying. I too
have started to send pictures
of myself out.

There was a time
when my father was dying.
He never sent out any pictures
to anyone, though. I did live
with him & I guess it wouldn't
have made sense to pay for
the postage.

When my father was dying,
I used to imagine his funeral
every night before I went
to sleep. He started dying
when I was eight & stopped
dying when I was twelve.
I imagined his funeral 1460
times.

Around the 1193rd time,
the third year, I stopped
crying. Writing "Do not bend:
Photographs enclosed" is
redundant.

"Fragile" is much shorter.

I teach freshman composition.
Every time the class concludes
I am upset that I am alone
in the room, packing my bag
with papers, books.

A part of me wishes
my students would stay
afterward to bask in afterglow,
to cuddle.

I figure out odd reasons
to call my parents late at night
while in bed. Last night,
I called my mother about
moths.

Fortunately, there is a time difference.

I ask them questions
I know the answers to.
I ask them questions that
I know they know
the answers to.

I do the same with students.

It's like leaving a wallet
at a lover's house, a reason
to return.

Will lavender ward away
these pestilent little things?
They put holes in wool.

Yes, and rosemary! Moths hate rosemary!

Did I tell you I bought
a new coat?

Two years ago, my step brother killed himself.

That's not true. It was
two years ago they found him—

in the woods. He'd driven
out into the Pacific
Northwest & drank
a bottle of Gatorade &
anti-freeze. Time
of departure becomes less
important than time
of arrival.

A plane ahead of schedule.

He left his suicide note
on a floppy disk.

My brother & I were pall-
bearers, my other brother
locked away 500 miles
south in a half-way house
in Koreatown.

We didn't know my step-brother
well. It was just that we were
the only ones who'd carry him.

At the wake, his two sons,
too small to carry
the casket, kicked a soccer-
ball against the church
wall, shaking the structure,
the congregation's
casseroles vibrating
on the fold out card tables.

They couldn't scrounge up
any recent photos
for the In Memoriam
Pamphlet they handed out
at the service.

The sick are not
photographed.

The only photograph,
the cover photograph,
was a photo of Steve when
he was nineteen, a soccer
ball underneath his left
cleat & Umbro shorts
kissing his thighs.

I call my father to tell him
I have a new coat,
a wool jobby like he had
in the navy— a pea-coat,
like the one in the photos
on Oahu's craggy shore.

I ask him if he still has his,
a question I know the answer.

Moths, a long time ago. Too bad, it was a good coat.

Lavender, I say.

If I had only known.

Before we hang up, I tell him
to expect a package.

He tells me the same.

Acknowledgments

Thank you to New Michigan Press for its publication of my chapbook *Your Daily Horoscope* in 2015, where many of these horoscopes also appeared. Thank you to the following publications in which some of these poems, in one form or another, were first published: *Omniverse*, *Southern Pacific Review*, *Fanzine*, *Dream Pop Press*, *Thermos*, *Public Pool*, *DIAGRAM*, *Sixth Finch*, and *Verse Daily*.

Thank you to my poem-a-day crew who makes sure that I actually do write something during the year: Justin Runge, Carrie Chappell, David Welch, Benjamin Sutton, Avni Janakrai Vyas, Jeremy Allan Hawkins, Michelle Burke, Brett Evans, and S. Whitney Holmes. Thank you to *Very Nice and Polite People* for all the dancing: Kristel Kovner, Michael Francesconi, Katy Pelissier, Ryan Gorman, and Joshua Rea. Thank you to my teachers for teaching me stuff: Mark Yakich, Molly Bendall, and Michael Martone. Thank you to Andrew Wessels for his friendship and tireless work with this book. Thank you to Elæ and everyone at The Operating System for making this book a book. And finally, thank you to my partner, Janna Knight — for all of it.

Essay / Assay: Acceptance, Perhaps
A Conversation with Nik De Dominic

Greetings! Thank you for talking to us about your process today! Can you introduce yourself, in a way that you would choose?

My name is Nik De Dominic. I am a poet and essayist. I am an editor of poetry for the *New Orleans Review*. I am originally from Los Angeles, California. I spent some time in Alabama, then New Orleans, Louisiana, and am now back in Los Angeles. I imagine there's some deeper significance in that: LA->AL->NOLA->LA. Or at least a chorus, a song.

I teach writing at the University of Southern California where I also co-direct the university's Prison Education Project. We offer faculty and student led courses at three correctional facilities in the region, as well as classes where USC students and students who are incarcerated are co-enrolled. We are also working towards creating re-entry resources at the university, a prison-to-college pipeline.

Why are you a poet/writer/artist?

This is a tough question. The whole questionnaire is. I either come off self-important or flip. Or, wait, what if I do approach the thing earnestly and people think I'm an idiot? Is now when I talk about generalized anxiety disorder?

Simplest answer - circular, I know - because I am. Here's where we play the Popeye theme.

When did you decide you were a poet/writer/artist (and/or: do you feel comfortable calling yourself a poet/writer/artist, what other titles or affiliations do you prefer/feel are more accurate)?

I drew as a kid. I still do but not well enough to actually do anything with it. Just well enough so when people see drawings, they go, oh, wow, that kind of looks like my dog; didn't know you could do that. But as a kid, I certainly thought I was going to be an artist. But today, I wouldn't call myself one.

I hesitate too to say I am a poet. Not because I don't think I am (it's different than the art thing; I actually publish this shit) but because when you call yourself a poet, meet someone at a party, people look at you like you're a wizard - some mystical other of a forgotten fantasy world. That or they think Def Poetry Jam (RIP Kanye): a stage, rhyme, rhythm. Stages I don't do and rhyme and rhythm, I don't have.

So, I say a writer. I'm ok with that. It invites the least interrogation.

What's a "poet" (or "writer" or "artist") anyway? What do you see as your cultural and social role (in the literary / artistic / creative community and beyond)?

I don't have those definitions and I think it up to the writer to define that for herself. Here, it's probably best to talk about my own shit. Many a wonderful poet and artist effect change with their work. I don't think of my work doing that: I write bad jokes.

What the work does allow me to do and its larger and social role is to keep a job at the university. The university then in turn grants me access to spaces and populations I wouldn't otherwise have access to. I get to work with students who are incarcerated; high school students; college students from all around Los Angeles, this country and this world, and others, and they in turn get to then go out and define those roles for themselves, as writers and artists and community members. I am incredibly grateful and humbled for that.

Talk about the process or instinct to move these poems (or your work in general) as independent entities into a body of work. How and why did this happen? Have you had this intention for a while? What encouraged and/or confounded this (or a book, in general) coming together? Was it a struggle?

Did you envision this collection as a collection or understand your process as writing or making specifically around a theme while the poems themselves were being written / the work was being made? How or how not?

I'm a terrible worker. And I need mechanisms to get things done, both in practice (actual writing of the things) and in content (horoscopes/ wolf poems - the exhaustion of that conceit drives the conceit).

I started the horoscope poems in '14 as a result of Poem-A-Day thing I do with a group of poets where we write (or at least try to) a poem a day for April and November. It was initially started to combat NaNoWriMo (why let fiction writers have all the fun). In '16 I began the *Wolf* poems in that same group.

I appreciate this archive project because if anyone were to anthologize my work say in 200 years, they'd have to footnote the shit out of it (what's BEJEWELED? Who's Miss Jackson?). Often I read contemporaries at like the big slicks (*Poetry, NYer* and the like) and there's a wonderful timeless time to the language (*The tree blossomed/hands cupped a blossom/blossom blossomed blossoms* — the pieces could've been written today, thirty years ago, or three hundred years ago). And I'm endlessly envious of those who can strip the today out of the work.

But in both the *Wolf* poems and the Horoscopes, my interest *is* the contemporary and a larger critique on consumption (perhaps even self-indictment: I'm chest deep in this shit). I consume. I work through news, Facebook feeds, my phone pings, and those things are central to the book. The theme is that — that and sickness. Disease is the other driver.

What formal structures or other constrictive practices (if any) do you use in the creation of your work? Have certain teachers or instructive environments, or readings/writings/work of other creative people informed the way you work/write?

The poem-a-day stuff mentioned above. Also, I studied with Michael Martone at Alabama and fuck, can that guy exhaust a thing. In fact, one of the classes he teaches is a 'hypoxic workshop' where the goal is to produce, produce and then produce some more. The final poem of the book is a result of that workshop. I was cheating his instruction: if the goal was to produce as many pages as possible, how can I do that w/out actually writing, I thought to myself. BOOM, tiny prose blocks! There are other writers, too, ones that live in the ear. Too many to count. Probably you.

Speaking of monikers, what does your title represent? How was it generated? Talk about the way you titled the book, and how your process of naming (individual pieces, sections, etc) influences you and/or colors your work specifically.

The title is about saying goodbye to disease. Letting go. Both in a sort of 'fuck it' but also in coming to terms with our mortality and failing bodies. Acceptance, perhaps.

I was diagnosed with Lupus in my late teens, early 20s. Cystic lung disease around 35. About two months ago I had open heart surgery to replace a failing aortic valve. And just yesterday, got word that the pulmonic valve replacement is faulty, that the fuckers have to go back in. OPEN HEART SURGERY II: THE RECKONING. It's a litany of sickness. All before 40.

But the thing is, I'm not really that sick. I've been lucky there. The wolf, here, then is the representation of that sickness — in all its terror. And, too, everydayness, its banality.

I see 4-6 doctors every 3 months. My wife, Janna, likes to say no news is good news. But blowing an hour at the cardiologist for her to say, shit's fine is frustrating. And then to do it again. And again.

The alternative however is the Saturday morning call when she's on call, "Mr. Demonic, I want to discuss the findings of your recent echo. I'm a bit concerned..."

What does this book DO (as much as what it says or contains)?

I think of poems as essays, or in the Montaigne sense, an assay; an attempt at understanding. These poems attempt to understand a contemporary condition - to find humor in it and to further explore the self.

What would be the best possible outcome for this book? What might it do in the world, and how will its presence as an object facilitate your creative role in your community and beyond? What are your hopes for this book, and for your practice?

Someone finds it funny.

About the Author

Nik De Dominic is an essayist and poet. Work has appeared in *Guernica*, *Los Angeles Review*, *DIAGRAM*, *Fairy Tale Review*, *Verse Daily* and elsewhere. De Dominic teaches writing at the University of Southern California where he also co-directs the university's Prison Education Program. He is the poetry editor of *New Orleans Review* and lives in Los Angeles.

WHY PRINT / DOCUMENT?

The Operating System uses the language "print document" to differentiate from the book-object as part of our mission to distinguish the act of documentation-in-book-FORM from the act of publishing as a backwards-facing replication of the book's agentive *role* as it may have appeared the last several centuries of its history. Ultimately, I approach the book as TECHNOLOGY: one of a variety of printed documents (in this case, bound) that humans have invented and in turn used to archive and disseminate ideas, beliefs, stories, and other evidence of production.

Ownership and use of printing presses and access to (or restriction of printed materials) has long been a site of struggle, related in many ways to revolutionary activity and the fight for civil rights and free speech all over the world. While (in many countries) the contemporary quotidian landscape has indeed drastically shifted in its access to platforms for sharing information and in the widespread ability to "publish" digitally, even with extremely limited resources, the importance of publication on physical media has not diminished. In fact, this may be the most critical time in recent history for activist groups, artists, and others to insist upon learning, establishing, and encouraging personal and community documentation practices. Hear me out.

With The OS's print endeavors I wanted to open up a conversation about this: the ultimately radical, transgressive act of creating PRINT /DOCUMENTATION in the digital age. It's a question of the archive, and of history: who gets to tell the story, and what evidence of our life, our behaviors, our experiences are we leaving behind? We can know little to nothing about the future into which we're leaving an unprecedentedly digital document trail — but we can be assured that publications, government agencies, museums, schools, and other institutional powers that be will continue to leave BOTH a digital and print version of their production for the official record. Will we?

As a (rogue) anthropologist and long time academic, I can easily pull up many accounts about how lives, behaviors, experiences — how THE STORY of a time or place — was pieced together using the deep study of correspondence, notebooks, and other physical documents which are no longer the norm in many lives and practices. As we move our creative behaviors towards digital note taking, and even audio and video, what can we predict about future technology that is in any way assuring that our stories will be accurately told – or told at all? How will we leave these things for the record?

In these documents we say:
WE WERE HERE, WE EXISTED, WE HAVE A DIFFERENT STORY

- Elæ [Lynne DeSilva-Johnson], Founder/Creative Director
THE OPERATING SYSTEM, Brooklyn NY 2018

RECENT & FORTHCOMING
OS PRINT::DOCUMENTS and PROJECTS, 2019-20

2020

Institution is a Verb: A Panoply Performance Lab Compilation
Poetry Machines: Letters for a Near Future - Margaret Rhee
My Phone Lies to me: Fake News Poetry Workshops as
Radical Digital Media Literacy - Alexandra Juhasz, Ed.
Goodbye Wolf-Nik DeDominic
Spite - Danielle Pafunda
Acid Western - Robert Balun
Cupping - Joseph Han

KIN(D)* TEXTS AND PROJECTS

Hoax - Joey De Jesus
#Survivor - Joanna C. Valente
Intergalactic Travels: Poems from a Fugitive Alien - Alan Pelaez Lopez
RoseSunWater - Angel Dominguez

GLOSSARIUM: UNSILENCED TEXTS AND TRANSLATIONS

Zugunruhe - Kelly Martinez Grandal (tr. Margaret Randall)
En el entre / In the between: Selected Antena Writings -
Antena Aire (Jen Hofer & John Pluecker)
Black and Blue Partition ('Mistry) - Monchoachi (tr. Patricia Hartland)
Si la musique doit mourir (If music were to die) -
Tahar Bekri (tr. Amira Rammah)
Farvernes Metafysik: Kosmisk Farvelære (The Metaphysics of Color: A Cosmic
Theory of Color) - Ole Jensen Nyrén (tr. Careen Shannon)
Híkurí (Peyote) - José Vincente Anaya (tr. Joshua Pollock)

2019

Ark Hive-Marthe Reed
I Made for You a New Machine and All it Does is Hope - Richard Lucyshyn
Illusory Borders-Heidi Reszies
A Year of Misreading the Wildcats - Orchid Tierney
Of Color: Poets' Ways of Making | An Anthology of Essays on Transformative Poetics - Amanda Galvan Huynh & Luisa A. Igloria, Editors

KIN(D)* TEXTS AND PROJECTS

A Bony Framework for the Tangible Universe-D. Allen
Opera on TV-James Brunton
Hall of Waters-Berry Grass
Transitional Object-Adrian Silbernagel

GLOSSARIUM: UNSILENCED TEXTS AND TRANSLATIONS

Śnienie / Dreaming - Marta Zelwan/Krystyna Sakowicz,
(Poland, trans. Victoria Miluch)
High Tide Of The Eyes - Bijan Elahi (Farsi-English/dual-language)
trans. Rebecca Ruth Gould and Kayvan Tahmasebian
In the Drying Shed of Souls: Poetry from Cuba's Generation Zero
Katherine Hedeen and Víctor Rodríguez Núñez, translators/editors
Street Gloss - Brent Armendinger with translations of Alejandro Méndez, Mercedes Roffé, Fabián Casas, Diana Bellessi, and Néstor Perlongher (Argentina)
Operation on a Malignant Body - Sergio Loo (Mexico, trans. Will Stockton)
Are There Copper Pipes in Heaven - Katrin Ottarsdóttir
(Faroe Islands, trans. Matthew Landrum)

2018

An Absence So Great and Spontaneous It Is Evidence of Light - Anne Gorrick
The Book of Everyday Instruction - Chloë Bass
Executive Orders Vol. II - a collaboration with the Organism for Poetic Research
One More Revolution - Andrea Mazzariello
Chlorosis - Michael Flatt and Derrick Mund
Sussuros a Mi Padre - Erick Sáenz
Abandoners - Lesley Ann Wheeler
Jazzercise is a Language - Gabriel Ojeda-Sague
Born Again - Ivy Johnson
Attendance - Rocío Carlos and Rachel McLeod Kaminer
Singing for Nothing - Wally Swist
Walking Away From Explosions in Slow Motion - Gregory Crosby
Field Guide to Autobiography - Melissa Eleftherion

KIN(D)* TEXTS AND PROJECTS

Sharing Plastic - Blake Nemec
The Ways of the Monster - Jay Besemer

GLOSSARIUM: UNSILENCED TEXTS AND TRANSLATIONS

The Book of Sounds - Mehdi Navid (Farsi dual language, trans. Tina Rahimi
Kawsay: The Flame of the Jungle - María Vázquez Valdez
(Mexico, trans. Margaret Randall)
Return Trip / Viaje Al Regreso - Israel Dominguez;
(Cuba, trans. Margaret Randall)

for our full catalog please visit:
https://squareup.com/store/the-operating-system/

deeply discounted Book of the Month and Chapbook Series subscriptions
are a great way to support the OS's projects and publications!
sign up at: http://www.theoperatingsystem.org/subscribe-join/

DOC U MENT
/däkyəmənt/

First meant "instruction" or "evidence," whether written or not.

noun - a piece of written, printed, or electronic matter that provides information or evidence or that serves as an official record
verb - record (something) in written, photographic, or other form
synonyms - paper - deed - record - writing - act - instrument

[Middle English, precept, from Old French, from Latin *documentum*, example, proof, from *docre*, to teach; see *dek-* in Indo-European roots.]

Who is responsible for the manufacture of value?

Based on what supercilious ontology have we landed in a space where we vie against other creative people in vain pursuit of the fleeting credibilities of the scarcity economy, rather than freely collaborating and sharing openly with each other in ecstatic celebration of MAKING?

While we understand and acknowledge the economic pressures and fear-mongering that threatens to dominate and crush the creative impulse, we also believe that
now more than ever we have the tools to relinquish agency via cooperative means,
fueled by the fires of the Open Source Movement.

Looking out across the invisible vistas of that rhizomatic parallel country we can begin to see our community beyond constraints, in the place where intention meets resilient, proactive, collaborative organization.

Here is a document born of that belief, sown purely of imagination and will. When we document we assert. We print to make real, to reify our being there. When we do so with mindful intention to address our process, to open our work to others, to create beauty in words in space, to respect and acknowledge the strength of the page we now hold physical, a thing in our hand, we remind ourselves that, like Dorothy: *we had the power all along, my dears.*

THE PRINT! DOCUMENT SERIES
is a project of
the trouble with bartleby
in collaboration with
`the operating system`

www.ingramcontent.com/pod-product-compliance
Lightning Source LLC
Chambersburg PA
CBHW022012120526
44592CB00034B/794